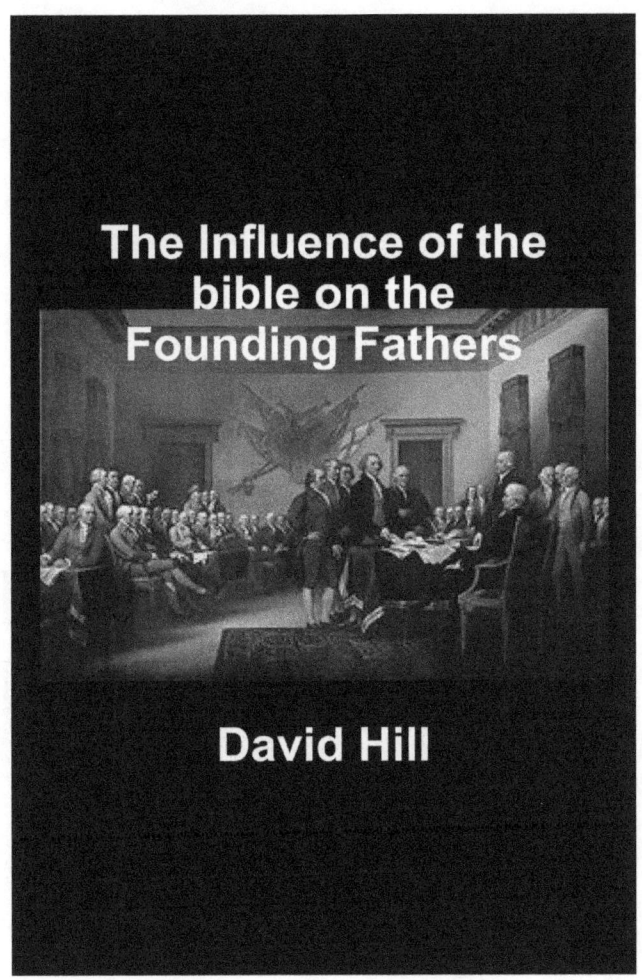

The Influence of the bible on the Founding Fathers

David Hill

The Influence of the Bible on

THE FOUNDING FATHERS

DAVID HILL

PUBLISHED BY FASTPENCIL, INC.

Copyright © 2011 David Hill

Published by FastPencil, Inc.
3131 Bascom Ave.
Suite 150
Campbell CA 95008 USA
(408) 540-7571
(408) 540-7572 (Fax)
info@fastpencil.com
http://www.fastpencil.com

The Publisher makes no representations or warranties with respect to the accuracy or completeness of the contents of this book and specifically disclaim any implied warranties of merchantability or fitness for a particular purpose. Neither the publisher nor author shall be liable for any loss of profit or any commercial damages.

First Edition

In Memory of My Grandfather Gilbert Lee Hill.
To Dwight and Judy Hill,
The State of Georgia
The United States of America

Acknowledgements

    And you shall ask me,
It will be my command:
    -you will ask for peace and I shall Give you a chance to make peace,
-you will ask for forgiveness and I shall give you a chance

The Influence of the Bible on the Founding Fathers

to forgive,
you will ask for my acceptance and I shall give you a chance
for you to accept others,
    All this I have done,
you shall do,
and so it shall be
(The day the Lord spoke to me)
~David Hill

Contents

Chapter 1	Found Fathers	1
Chapter 2	References	73

1

Found Fathers

America's founding settlers and Founding Fathers were largely considered Christian, not Deists; and the influence of the Bible on the founding of America had a direct and dramatic influence on the documents and form of government that developed the framework for the "longest running constitutional republic in history." The influence of Christianity on the lives around the world over thousands of years has not only been a staple in the way that individuals conduct their lives but has more been a set of principles and philosophies in building the foundation of our government, law, education, our economic system and many other aspects. While America is struggling economically and socially, many historians are trying to rewrite history to conform to what many have on their agenda to conform to the appeasement of being politically correct. So in order to understand the viability of a successful future for America it is important to firmly establish and adhere to principles of the past and to carry them forward for future generations. In general conversation with individuals on this topic it seems to be one with varying ideas, passions and beliefs but only the facts of history can prove the course to preserve our past to ensure the future.

The influence of the Bible on America can clearly be seen dating from 1620 when the pilgrims and puritans first landed in Massachusetts. Yale Professor (1955-1986) and noted historian Edmund Morgan, in his book *The*

Puritan Dilemma: The Story of John Winthrop, put it this way, "Rulers, however selected, received their authority from God, not from the people, and were accountable to God, not to the people." "England in 1534 broke away from the Roman Catholic Church and created the Church of England. During this time since there was no separation of Church and state everyone had to belong to the Church of England. The separatists wanted to separate from the Church of England. William Bradford the leader of the separatist and followers decided to leave England and start a settlement of their own so that they could practice their religion freely. The Virginia Company gave Bradford permission to establish a new colony in Virginia. The Pilgrims set sail on the Mayflower in September 1620 towards Virginia." The Puritans wanted to originally purify and reform the Church but as a result of their inability to do so, many of the followers came to America to have religious freedoms. The religious freedoms that both the Pilgrims and Puritans were seeking would ultimately have a direct influence on the formation of America. Below is a copy of the embarkation of the pilgrims in the U.S capital.

…Embarkation of the Pilgrims was painted by Robert Weir. The Pilgrims are shown kneeling on the deck of their ship in 1620 as they depart for America from Holland. William Brewster holds an open Bible, while Pastor John Robinson leads Governor Carver, William Bradford, Miles Standish, and the Pilgrim families in prayer. The open Bible was the Geneva Bible, favored by the Pilgrims and early Puritans.

During the same time period that the Pilgrims landed, Virginia had their first state elected legislature in 1620.

The Pilgrims, Puritans and other groups of people that made the venture to the New World for centuries had relied on the established historical practice of a Monarchy or King rule being the head of the religion. This new freedom coming to the New World gave many new comers the chance for the first time to not only read the Bible without restrictions from the English monarch but to take the language in the text to heart and act on the direct meaning for the first time without the king or "direct ruler from God" of kings who many considered as always passing judgment on the people. During this period, as it had been seen for many previous centuries, the religion of the people was at the sole discretion of whatever the religion of the King was at the time. People during the 1620s-1650's who wanted to come to the New World for religious freedoms wanted to make sure they would never experience oppression of being told who was allowed to be educated in the scripture of the Bible. This fear was first realized and put to rest through a piece of legislation in Connecticut in 1647. The law of 1647 was often referred to as the old deluder. The Code of 1650 states:

It being one chief project of that old deluder, Satan, to keep men from the knowledge of the Scriptures, as in former times keeping them in an unknown tongue, so in these later times by perswading from the use of tongues, that so at least the true sense and meaning of the Originall might be clowded by false glosses of Saint-seeming deceivers; and that learning may not be buried in the graves of our fore-fathers in Church and Commonwealth, the Lord assisting our indeavors: it is therefore ordered by this Court and Authoritie therof; that every Township in this Jurisdiction, after the Lord hath increased them to the number of fifty Housholders, shall then forthwith appoint one within their town to teach all such children as shall resort to him to write and read, whose wages shall be paid either by the Parents or Masters of such children, or by the Inhabitants in general, by way of supply, as the major part of those that order the prudentials of the Town shall appoint. Provided that those which send their children be not oppressed by paying much more then they can have them taught for in other towns.

And it is further ordered, that where any town shall increase to the number of one hundred Families or Housholders, they shall set up a Grammar-School, the Masters thereof being able to instruct youth so far as they may be fitted for the Universitie. And if any town neglect the performance hereof above one year then everie such town shall pay five pounds per annum to the next such School, till they shall perform this Order. [1647]

Not only does this language give the citizens assurance that the Bible will not be taken from them, it reassures that the Bible will be taught in the school. Another line of reference in the above passage to take notice of is…"in church and commonwealth the Lord assisting our endeavors"…This is giving direct credit in the Code of 1650 law to God as the principle source of inspiration for their guidance and direction.

The example below is another instance of the people's case in point where the Bible would not be taken away from the people and their reliance for it to be practiced in the schools. Below is an illustration of the first school book published in Connecticut, which was called the New England Primer. In this text book it clearly established the founding necessity of religion to be taught in school. One can clearly see in the pictures the references to both God and to Jesus Christ.

Both of the pictures below are clear examples of the first textbook published:

The next example of the necessity and value of pray can be seen in the early legislative branch of the government in the Continental Congress.

CONTINENTAL CONGRESS

On the opening of the Continental Congress on September 6, 1774, the following resolution was presented "Resolved, that the Reverend Mr.Duche` be desired to open congress tomorrow morning with prayers, at the Carpenter's hall." This opening prayer of the Continental Congress was declared to be…'worth riding one hundred mile to hear, even Quakers shed tears." In a letter From John Adams to Abigail Adams regarding the first prayer in congress the future president writes:

I never saw a greater effect upon an audience. It seemed as if Heaven had ordained that Psalm to be read on that morning.

After this, Mr. Duche, unexpectedly to everybody, struck out into an extemporary prayer, which filled the bosom of every man present. I must confess, I never heard a better prayer, or one so well pronounced. Episcopalian as he is, Dr. Cooper himself never prayed with such fervor, such ardor, such earnestness and pathos, and in language so elegant and sublime, for America, for the Congress, for the province of Massachusetts Bay, and especially the town of Boston.

It can clearly been seen in the opening of the Continental Congress that the Word of the Lord and the Bible were very much fundamental parts of the daily practices of not only the men, but that of the ideas the men implemented to create the American government. There were many Founding Fathers that held an instrumental religious faith which was the basis long before the two famous American documents were written; the Declaration of independence and the Constitution. Discussed in detail are many of these Founding Fathers and their own writings that support their faith and the clear example they carried over in the founding documents. The First Founding Father in the research to be discussed is John Hancock.

JOHN HANCOCK

One of the possibilities, even though John Hancock lost his father at a very young age of seven, for the reinforcement of his religious beliefs could have been the fact that his father was a Puritan minister. Later on in Mr. Hancock's life he would say in his Inaugural Address as Governor of Massachusetts,

A due observation of the Lord's Day is not only important to internal religion, but greatly conducive to the order and benefit of civil society. It speaks to the senses of mankind, and, by a solemn cessation from their common affairs, reminds them of a Deity and their accountableness to the great Lord of all. Whatever may be necessary to the support of such an institution, in consistence with a reasonable personal liberty, deserves the attention of civil government." Manners, by which not only the freedom, but the very existences of the republics, are greatly affected, depend much upon the public institutions of religion and the good education of the youth.

The previous statement in his speech proves the continued to emphasize the importance of religion, as on ongoing institution.

JOHN ADAMS

John Adams was another Founding Father who was a signer of the Declaration of Independence. His beliefs in the Bible can be seen in the passage below:

The General principles on which the fathers achieved independence were...the general principles of Christianity. Now I will avow that I then believed, and now believe, that those general principles of Christianity are as eternal and immutable as the existence and attributes of God.

John Adams had a distinguished list of accomplishment throughout his career. He was first admitted to the Massachusetts Bar in 1761. Next he was elected to the Massachusetts Assembly in 1770. During the years of 1774-1776 he attended the First Continental Congress and signed the Declaration of Independence in 1776. He was also appointed Diplomat to France during the years 1776 to 1779. John Adams was also a member of the assembly to form the State Constitution of Massachusetts. He was the Minister plenipotentiary in Europe from 1780 through 1781. He was an instrumental part of the Treaty of Peace with Great Britain in 1783. He was then appointed as the United States Minister to the British court and served from 1783 to 1788. In 1789 he was elected Vice

President of the United States. John Adams becomes President of the United States in 1796. Below is a letter written to Thomas Jefferson on December 8th 1818 from John Adams showing his commitment to the necessity of God as part of his philosophical and spiritual beliefs:

I believe in God and in his Wisdom and Benevolence: and I cannot conceive that such a Being could make such a Species as the human merely to live and die on this Earth. If I did not believe a future State I should believe in no God. This Un[i]verse; this all; this **τοπαν** [.totality.]; would appear with all its swelling Pomp, a boyish Fire Work.

The continued writings of spiritual practices of God and the Lord can be seen clearly in the next Founding Father Benjamin Rush.

Benjamin Rush is a less known Founding Father but a very brilliant and influential person in history. Like John Adams, Benjamin Rush was a signer of the Declaration of Independence and a member of the first Continental Congress. Dr. Rush was at the convention where the constitution was ratified in Pennsylvania. He was a Professor and treasurer of the U.S. mint until his death in 1797. Dr. Rush was more directly a proponent of the necessity of the Bible on the influence of doctrine and in the formation of the American government. This can clearly be seen in Dr. Rush's work titled Essays in the chapter titled,' "Defense of the Bible as a School Book," addressed to the Rev. Jeremy Belknap, of Boston:(the entire section pg 93-113 is filled with additional references)

1) The chriftianity is the only true and perfect religion and that in proportion as mankind adopt its principles, and obey its precepts, they will be wife, and happy.

2) That a better knowledge of this religion is to be acquired by reading the bible, than in other way.

3) The Bible contains more knowledge neceffary to man in his prefent, than any other book in the world.

The next Founding Father that will be discussed is Robert Treat pain. His pledge to the Christian Faith and Jesus can clearly be seen in his own writings.

ROBERT TREAT PAINE

Robert Treat Paine was another influential statesman who was Biblically centered. Robert Paine served as a chaplain in the French and Indian war but gave up his ministry for law. He was not one to propose many new ideas but often opposed everything that was said in discussion. Dr.Benjamin Rush was once quoted as saying about Robert Treat Paine, " ..[he] is "the Object Maker", because he "seldom proposed anything, but apposed nearly every measure that was proposed by other people..." He was well known for his prosecution of the British troops indicted for murder during the Boston massacre, whereas; John Adam defended the British troops. He was a signer of the Declaration of Independence. His religious commitment can clearly been seen in one of his famous quotes:

I am constrained to express my adoration of the Supreme Being, the Author of my existence, in full belief of His providential goodness and His forgiving mercy revealed to the world through Jesus Christ, through Whom I hope for neverending happiness in a future state.

Robert Paine, during the years of 1774-1778 served as a member of the Continental Congress. In 1775 he was sent (with John Langdon and **Robert** R. Livingston) on an unsuccessful mission to win Canada to the Revolutionary cause. **Paine** later served as attorney general of Massachusetts and then (1790–1804) as state Supreme Court justice. In 1776 he was one of the signers of the Declaration of independence. The next Founding Father to be discussed in this research is Charles Carroll. He is one of the most overlooked of the Founding Father, as having a major impact of the formation of the documents and philosophy that built the United States.

CHARLES CARROLL

Charles Carroll was another influential Founding Father who is not remembered today as he should be. Charles Carroll was born on September 20, 1737 in Maryland. "He was sent to France, at the age of eight to obtaining his education. He attended the college of English Jesuits, at St. Omer's, where he studied for six years." The English Jesuits School that he attended was a Catholic school that focus heavily on the teaching of Catholicism. He was not very interested in politics at the start and concentrated most of time on the practice of law. Faced with both persecution and restrictions for his faith, Charles Carroll of Carrollton embodied his family's vision of personal, political and religious freedom for all citizens when he became the only Catholic to sign the Declaration of Independence in 1776. His faith can be evidenced by his proclamation, "On the mercy of my Redeemer I rely for salvation, and on His merits; not on the works that I have done in obedience to His precepts." Charles Carroll had more to lose than many of the Founding Fathers if the colonies were unable to separate themselves from the rule of the British. Charles Carroll stated:

Without morals a republic cannot subsist any length of time; they therefore who are decrying the Christian religion, whose morality is so sublime & pure, [and] which denounces against the wicked eternal misery, and [which] insured to the good eternal happiness, are undermining the solid foundation of morals, the best security for the duration of free governments.

His fortune was estimated at over $2,000,000. He was considered one the wealthiest men in the colonies if not the wealthiest man. He died in 1832. He was the oldest surviving signer of the declaration of independence, passing away at the age of 95. Our next Founding Father John Witherspoon had one of the most fundamental understandings of the scripture and the necessity of scripture to be a guiding principle of the founding of America.

JOHN WITHERSPOON

"John Witherspoon was born in the parish of Yester near Scotland on February 5, on 1722. He was a direct descendant of the great reformer, John Knox. His beloved father was a minister in the Scottish church, at Yester. His father took great interest to John's need for an early education. John's father wanted the education of sound moral and religious principles taught to him. He very much wanted John to be in the gospel ministry. John Witherspoon received his primary education in Haddington. At the young age of 14 John was placed in the University of Edinburgh. To the delight of his father, John focused upom sacred literature. John went through a regular theological course of study, and at the age of twenty- two years he graduated, a licensed preacher." The study of the "sacred literature" in the case of John Witherspoon is just one of many examples of the role religious views influenced the founding documents of America. John Witherspoon expresses his sentiment on Government with the statement below:

To promote true religion is the best and most effectual way of making a virtuous and regular people. Love to God and love to man is the substance of religion; when these prevail, civil laws will have little to do. ... The magistrate (or ruling part of any society) ought to encourage piety... [and] make it an object of public esteem. Those who are vested with civil authority ought ... to promote religion and good morals among all their government.

In one of his lectures titled "Lectures on Moral Philosophy" he states:

An oath is an appeal to God, the Searcher of hearts, for the truth of what we say and always expresses or supposes an imprecation of His judgment upon us if we prevaricate. An oath, therefore, implies a belief in God and His Providence and indeed is an act of worship. ... Persons entering on public offices are also often obliged to make oath that they will faithfully execute their trust. ... In vows, there is no party but God and the person himself who makes the vow.

John Witherspoon obviously had a profound inherent belief of God that translated into his philosophy as a statesman. In the early part of 1776, he was asked to assist in the formation of a new Constitution for New Jersey. His patriotic sentiments and sound judgment were the main reason, in June that year in

1776, he was elected a delegate to the General Congress. He had already formed a decided opinion in favor of Independence, and he gave his support to the resolution declaring the States free forever. On June 29, 1776 he took his seat in congress. On July 1st, when the subject of the Declaration of Independence was discussed, a distinguished member remarked, that "the people are not ripe for a Declaration of Independence." Doctor Witherspoon observed: "In my judgment, sir, we are not only ripe, but rotting." On the second of August 1776 he signed his name on the Declaration of Independence. He died on November 15, 1794 (age 71) near Princeton New Jersey.

GEORGE WASHINGTON

The most famous of the Founding Fathers was George Washington. George Washington was born on the morning of February 22, 1732 into a modest plantation in Virginia. When George was 11 years old, his father died, leaving only a modest inheritance for his wife and children. Because there was no money to send George away to school, his formal education ended when he was just 14. At age 12, Washington copied down <u>110 Rules of Civility and Decent Behavior in Company & Conversation</u>. He wrote these down to show his visions of becoming a Virginia gentleman. Washington was raised in the Church of Virginia, as well as baptized in the same Church. Martha, Washington's wife was a dedicated Anglican and attended church of a regular basis. Washington attended Church about as much as other people during the same time period. As a military leader since he did not have a chaplin,

Washington relegated himself to read the Gospel to his soldiers. Below is Washington famous prayer at Valley Forge:

Almighty and eternal Lord God, the great Creator of heaven and earth, and the God and Father of our Lord Jesus Christ; look down from heaven in pity and compassion upon me Thy servant, who humbly prorate myself before Thee.

There are more quotes of religious faith and practices from George Washington than just about any of the other Founding Fathers. There were many times where the Lord heard his call for help and saved him, either at Valley Forge, or one of his many battles where he was shot through his clothes and never wounded. Washington's diary indicates that he worshiped more frequently during national crises and periods of residence in cities, where

churches were more accessible than they were from Mount Vernon. The assistant rector of Christ Church attested to Washington's "regular attendance" when the capital was in Philadelphia. "The next quote shows a personal touch into the life of George Washington's churchgoing in New York City. "The President of the United States presents his Compliments to Mr. Jay," a note from Washington to John jay in 1789 declares, and informs him that Harness of the President's carriage was so much injured in coming from New Jersey that he will not be able to use it to-day. If Mr. Jay should propose going to Church this morning the President would be obliged to him for a seat in his carriage. It's interesting to get this type of historical view where the President is asking for a ride to Church. The wording of Washington's letter sounds as if there might be

a chance the President of the United States cannot get a ride. Clearly there are times in Washington's life and in his journals where he does not attend church every week. Regardless of his attendance it is evident that President Washington's religious beliefs were a guiding principle in his life. Below is an example of Washington's writing showing his obedience to God. This letter was sent to 13 Governors on June 14, 1783:

I now make it my earnest prayer that God would have you, and the State over which you preside, in his holy protection; that he would incline the hearts of the citizens to cultivate a spirit of subordination and obedience to government, to entertain a brotherly affection and love for one another, for their fellow-citizens of the United States at large, and particularly for brethren who have served in the field; and finally that he would most graciously be pleased to dispose us all to do justice, to love mercy, and to demean ourselves with that charity, humility, and pacific temper of mind, which were the characteristics of the Divine Author of our blessed religion, and without an humble imitation of whose example in these things, we can never hope to be a happy nation.

There have been authors that make the case that President Washington was a deist. Based on the research it is very difficult for one to come to the conclusion that Washington could even be close to a deist. There can be no doubt that even though President Washington in many times in his life did not always follow the same religious strictness in practices as other people, he still had a very close and personal relationship with God. This is a famous Prayer from George Washington professing his faith:

Most Gracious Lord God, from whom proceedeth every good and perfect gift, I offer to Thy divine majesty my unfeigned praise & thanksgiving for Thy mercies towards me. Thou mad'st me at first and hast ever since sustained the work of Thy own hand; Thou gav'st Thy Son to die for me, and hast given me assurance of salvation, upon my repentance and sincerely endeavoring to conform my life to His holy precepts and example. Thou art pleased to lengthen out to me the time of repentance and to move me to it by Thy Spirit and Thy Word, by Thy mercies, and by Thy judgments; out of a deepness of Thy mercies, and my own unworthiness,..

..I do appear before Thee at this time; I have sinned and done very wickedly, be merciful to me, O God, and pardon me for Jesus Christ's sake; instruct me in the particulars of my duty, and suffer me not to be tempted above what thou givest me strength to bear.

The above passage is a clear indication of the need for God in Washington's life and the continued reliance on the Lords ability to forgive and show him direction. To disprove Washington as a deist he must not consider God and the Lord's continued spirits an ongoing presents in one's life. This Quote proves that Washington is not a deist.

Take care, I pray thee of my affairs and more and more direct me in Thy truth, defend me from my enemies, especially my spiritual ones. Suffer me not to be drawn from Thee, by the blandishments of the world, carnal desires, the cunning of the devil, or deceitfulness of sin. Work in me Thy good will and pleasure and discharge my mind from all things that are displeasing to Thee, of all ill will and discontent, wrath and bitterness, pride & vain conceit of myself, and render me charitable, pure, holy, patient and heavenly minded. Be with me at the hour of death; dispose me for it, and deliver me from the slavish fear of it, and make me willing and fit to die whenever Thou shouldst call me hence. Bless our rulers in church and state. Bless O Lord the whole race of mankind, and let the world be filled with the knowledge of Thee and Thy Son Jesus Christ. Pity the sick, the poor, the weak, the needy, the widows and fatherless, and all that morn or are broken in heart, and be merciful to them according to their several necessities. Bless my friends and grant me grace to forgive my enemies as heartily as I desire forgiveness of Thee my heavenly Father....

The section below shows more evidence of Washington's continued need for God's Grace in his life as a continued presence.

...I beseech Thee to defend me this night from all evil, and do more for me than I can ask or think, for Jesus Christ sake, in whose most holy name & words, I continue to pray, Our Father &c.

Washington was elected as the first President of the United States and was a signer of the Constitution. [Washington was in New York preparing to defend Manhattan against the British when the Declaration of Independence was signed.] President Washington was considered the richest person in the United States. His net worth was consider to be half a billion dollars in today's money. President Washington died in Mount Vernon on December 14, 1799. George Washington was a true man of morals, character, leadership, love of country and an example for many generations to come. The next

Founding Father, James McHenry was an immigrant who had a positive impact On America from his views of scripture.

JAMES MCHENRY

James McHenry was born in Ireland in 1753. He came to the United States in 1771 at the age of 18. He had a typical classical education of the time. An example of his religious affiliation can clearly be seen in the fact that he was founder of the Baltimore Bible Society and was its president. The religious beliefs that he developed over the years could have been reinforced by one of his early teachers and Dr. Benjamin Rush or under having served with George Washington at Valley Forge. McHenry served as Secretary of War from 1796 to 1800 under both George Washington and John Adams. Fort McHenry was best known for its role in the Battle of Baltimore, successfully staved off the British invasion of the fort by 1,000 Americans that inspired Francis Scott Key, a lawyer and amateur poet, to compose the Star Spangled Banner, originally entitled Defense of Fort McHenry. In the below quote James McHenry expresses his view of Holy scripture:

[P]ublic utility pleads most forcibly for the general distribution of the Holy Scriptures. The doctrine they preach, the obligations they impose, the punishment they threaten, the rewards they promise, the stamp and image of divinity they bear, which produces a conviction of their truths, can alone secure to society, order and peace, and to our courts of justice and constitutions of government, purity, stability and usefulness. In vain, without the Bible, we increase penal laws and draw entrenchments around our institutions. Bibles are strong entrenchments. Where they abound, men cannot pursue wicked courses, and at the same time enjoy quiet conscience.

Clearly this quote shows the necessity of the Bible's role in society and the value of the written scripture to keep man pure and pure of immoral actions.

McHenry missed many of the proceedings at the Philadelphia convention, in part because of the illness of his brother, and played an insubstantial part in the debates when he was present. He did, however, maintain a private journal that has been useful to posterity. He campaigned strenuously for the Constitution in Maryland and attended the state ratifying convention.'

James McHenry remained a loyal Federalist until his death at the age of 62 in 1816. The Next founding father, Abraham

Baldwin was instrumental in the founding of America and the University of Georgia Educational system.

ABRAHAM BALDWIN

Abraham Baldwin another Founding Father and signer of the Declaration of Independence who was also the principle founder of the University of Georgia. Abraham Baldwin was the founder of the University of Georgia, as well as, a delegate to the Constitutional Convention in 1787. Abraham Baldwin was born on November 22, 1754, to Lucy Dudley and Michael Baldwin in North Guilford, Connecticut. His father was a blacksmith who had twelve children by two wives. Baldwin's father borrowed money to send his son to Yale College (later Yale University.) in New Haven, Connecticut. At Yale Baldwin studied theology and prepared for a career as a minister before the tumultuous years of the American Revolution (1775-83).

Once again the research provides overwhelming evidence of yet another Founding Father who was educated in the Gospel and had prepared and studied as a minister. These inherent moral beliefs they developed through theological education of Christianity carried forward not only as a Founding Father but in the pursuit of his desire for higher education which lead him to develop the education plan for Georgia as a representative of the state. This quote shows us the direct relationship that both religion and education had on his founding principles:

When the minds of the people in general are viciously disposed and unprincipled, and their conduct disorderly, a free-government, will be attended with greater confusions and evils more horrid than the wild, uncultivated state of nature. It can only be happy when the public principle and opinions are properly directed and their manners regulated. This is an influence beyond the reach of laws and punishments and can be claimed only by religion and education.

Baldwin was one of the four Georgia delegates to the constitutional convention of 1787. Three of the additional representatives were: William Few Jr., William Houston, and William Pierce. Baldwin and William Few were the only Georgia delegates to sign the Constitution. One of the more important contributions Baldwin made was the idea of representation from the smaller states to the national Senate. His ideas brought about the instrumental change of bringing about the compromise that established representation in both the House of Representatives and the Senate based on population.

Baldwin himself considered his role in the so-called Great Compromise of the Constitutional convention to be his greatest public service. Along with his greatest accomplishment to public service in being instrumental in the establishment of representation in government, once again it is evidenced in this quote the value of religion on the school system:

It should therefore be among the first objects of those who wish well to the national prosperity to encourage and support the principles of religion and morality, and early to place the youth under the forming hand of society, that by instruction they may be molded to the love of virtue and good order.

In the University of Georgia Charter, 1785, one can visibly see the religious influence he had on the school:

...9th ALL OFFICERS appointed to the instruction, and government of the University, shall be of the Christian Religion, and within three months after they enter upon the execution of their Trust, shall publicly take the Oath of Allegiance and Fidelity, and the Oaths of office prescribed in the Statutes of the University the President, before the Governor or President of Council, and all other Officers, before the President of the University.

11th THE TRUSTEES shall not exclude any person of any religious denomination, whatsoever, from free, and equal liberty, and advantages of education, or from any of the Liberties Priviledges and Immunities of the University in his education, on account of his or their speculative sentiments in Religion or being of different Religious Profession.

On March 4, 1807, at age fifty-three, Baldwin died while serving as a U.S. senator from Georgia. He is buried in Washington's Rock Creek Cemetery. The Next Founding Father is Gouverneur Morris.

GOUVERNEUR MORRIS

In researching Gouverneur Morris it has been mentioned in multiple locations where people have taken the position he was a deist. Having researched him, there is a lack of institutional Biblical training like we see with many of the Founding Fathers. It is important to clearly define deism to disprove the myth he was a deist. Deism "is the belief in the existence of a God on the evidence of reason and nature only, with rejection of supernatural revelation (distinguished from theism).2.belief in a God who created the world but has since remained indifferent to it." The fact he would not be considered a deist can be proved by Gouverneur Morris's quote on the Bible:

The reflection and experience of many years have led me to consider the holy writings not only as the most authentic and instructive in themselves, but as the clue to all other history. They tell us what man is, and they alone tell us why he is what he is: a contradictory creature that seeing and approving of what is good, pursues and performs what is evil. All of private and public life is there displayed. ... From the same pure fountain of wisdom we learn that vice destroys freedom; that arbitrary power is founded on public immorality.

In the first definition of deism when it states "with rejection of supernatural revelation" and in the second definition, "created the world but has since remained indifferent to it", that can clearly be disproved in his quote with the phrase, "authentic and instructive in themselves." The phrase "authentic and instructive in themselves" clearly gives daily instruction disproving deist on the notion of the definition "but has remained indifferent to it." If one interprets a daily direction through the Bible clearly the scripture cannot be indifferent.

Gouvernuer Morris was regarded as one of the brightest of men to serve during this time, excelling in all academics. He must have felt that the need for education and for religion to be combined in this famous quote, "Religion is the only solid basis of good morals; therefore education should teach the precepts of religion and the duties of man toward God." Gouverneur Morris also made a plea disproving the definition of deism in a famous quote about the role of religion in the government. Again, in this example one can clearly see that religion is a daily guiding course or principles and morality, for avoiding the extremes of despotism or anarchy... the only ground of hope must be on the morals of the people. I believe that religion is the only solid base of morals and that morals are the only possible support of free governments."

One of Gouverneur Morris's more famous contributions to the Constitution were the words "We the People of the United States, in order to form a more perfect Union." He was in charge of the committee to submit the final draft of the document and had a large role in the construction. In his last years he was disappointed with the new group of political leaders and the new philosophy of government. He died November 6, 1816.

WILLIAM PATTERSON

William Paterson like some of the other Founding Fathers did not have a formal background in the pursuits of ministry.

He was in the small number of Founding Fathers that had a chance to sign the Constitution. There could possibly be a misconception that all of the Founding Fathers were from America. William Paterson was born in Ireland like another Founding Father mentioned previously, James McHenry. William Patterson was one of the nine Constitutional signers who were foreign born. He came to American two years after he was born in 1747. Like many of the Founding Fathers he was highly educated for the time. He had both a B.A. and received a M.A three years later. He would go on to study and practice law similar to other Founding Fathers of the time. This Proclamation below was printed in the Gazette of the United States, November 26, 1791. This was the first example in the research where a Founding Father has made a declaration of a pray day, which was to be Thanksgiving Day praise to "almighty Ruler of the Universe."

Proclamation:

Whereas it is, at all times, our duty to approach the throne of Almighty God with gratitude and praise, but more especially in seasons of national peace, plenty, and prosperity; I have, therefore, thought fit, by and with the advice and consent of the Honorable the Privy Council, to assign Thursday the eighth day of December next, to be set apart and observed as a day of Public Thanksgiving and Prayer for the great and manifold mercies conferred upon this land and people; and particularly for the abundant produce of the earth, during the present year, for the spirit of industry, sobriety, and economy which prevails: for the stability and extension of our national credit and commerce, for the progress of literature, arts and science, and for the good order, peace and plenty, and the civil and religious liberty with which we are blessed. And also that we may unite in our supplications, and humbly implore the Almighty Ruler of the Universe, that he would be pleased to continue his protection and goodness to this land and people, to smile upon all schools and seminaries of learning; to promote agriculture, manufactures and commerce, to illuminate and guide our public councils, to bless our national and state governments, to enable us all to discharge our official, social and relative duties with diligence and fidelity, to eradicate prejudice, bigotry and superstition; to advance the interest of religion, and the knowledge and practice of virtue; and for this purpose to pour out his holy spirit on all ministers of the gospel, and to spread the saving light thereof to the most distant parts of the earth.

Given under my hand and seal at arms, at Trenton, the twenty-first day of November, in the year of our Lord one thousand seven hundred and ninety-one.

William Paterson in the above proclamation does not use the words Lord or Christ but in the defense of him not being a deist it breaks the definition of being a deist. In the definition given under Founding Father Gouverneur Morris's section, the second part of the definition clearly states, "belief in a God who created the world but has since remained indifferent to it." Creating a day of Prayer is not consistent with the Deist Definition of "remained indifferent to it." It clearly show that 'Almighty Ruler of the Universe' still has a divine hand in the faith and oversight of the people and the outcomes of their lives. William Patterson in 1789 was elected to the United States Senate. He played a critical role in drafting the Judiciary

Act of 1789. His next position from 1790-1793 was the Governor of New Jersey. During this time he started working on a set of documents that he later published as Laws of the State of New Jersey in 1800. He also began to revise the rules and practices of the court of England and common law courts to fit the United States Philosophy of law. During the years 1793-1806, Paterson served as an associate justice of the U.S. Supreme Court. Riding the grueling circuit to which federal judges were subjected in those days and sitting with the full Court, he presided over a number of major trials." He passed away at the age of sixty due to a decline in his health.

PATRICK HENRY

Patrick Henry was born into a Virginia family on May 29, 1736. He was one of the very few Founding Fathers that had no real formal education. He was what is referred to today as homeschooled by his father and later went on to teach himself law. He then went to take the law exam and as history records the rest is history. The son of an Anglican Vestryman and the nephew of an Anglican rector, Patrick Henry was strongly influenced by an evangelical leader of the great Awakening. An active Episcopalian, he read the Bible daily, paid for the printing and distribution of two attacks on Deism by British authors, and distributed religious tracts while riding circuit as a lawyer. His letters and addresses typically spoke of "All mighty God," "the gospel of Jesus," and "the merits of Jesus." In his last words he expressed gratitude to God. His will declared that, "religion of Christ" would give his family the inheritance "which will make them rick indeed." Henry would clearly be classified as an orthodox Christian. Patrick Henry was one of the most vocal proponents against the British rule. Mr. Henry pushed the envelope many times with his outspoken views against the British, which many people considered to be treasonous. One of his most famous speeches can be seen below. Please note the six different biblical references as additional proof of his strong Christian faith.

Give Me Liberty Or Give Me Death" Patrick Henry - 03/23/1775

No man thinks more highly than I do of the patriotism, as well as abilities, of the very worthy gentlemen who have just addressed the House. But different men often see the same subject in different lights; and, therefore, I hope it will not be thought disrespectful to those gentlemen if, entertaining as I do opinions of a character very opposite to theirs, I shall speak forth my sentiments freely and without reserve. This is no time for ceremony. The questing before the House is one of awful moment to this country. For my own part, I consider it as nothing less than a question of freedom or slavery; and in proportion to the magnitude of the subject ought to be the freedom of the debate. It is only in this way that we can hope to arrive at truth, and fulfill the great responsibility which we hold to God and our country.

The last sentence in this speech is him giving credit to God by the necessity of being held responsible to God and the country.

Should I keep back my opinions at such a time, through fear of giving offense, I should consider myself as guilty of treason towards my country, and of an act of disloyalty toward the Majesty of Heaven, which I revere above all earthly kings.

Mr. President, it is natural to man to indulge in the illusions of hope. We are apt to shut our eyes against a painful truth, and listen to the song of that siren till she transforms us into beasts. Is this the part of wise men, engaged in a great and arduous struggle for liberty? Are we disposed to be of the number of those who, having eyes, see not, and, having ears, hear not, the things which so nearly concern their temporal salvation?

This last sentence is a direct passage from the bible. It comes from Jeremiah 5:21, "hear this, O foolish and senseless people, who have eyes, but see not, who have ears, but hear not.

For my part, whatever anguish of spirit it may cost, I am willing to know the whole truth; to know the worst, and to provide for it. I have but one lamp by which my feet are guided, and that is the lamp of experience. I know of no way of judging of the future but by the past. And judging by the past, I wish to know what there has been in the conduct of the British ministry for the last ten years to justify those hopes with which gentlemen have been pleased to solace themselves and the House. Is it that insidious smile with which our petition has been lately received? Trust it not, sir; it will prove a snare to your feet. Suffer not yourselves to be betrayed with a kiss

This last sentence can be traced directly to the Bible. It can be found in Mathew 26:48 and states, "..The one I shall kiss is the man; seize him."

Ask yourselves how this gracious reception of our petition comports with those warlike preparations which cover our waters and darken our land. Are fleets and armies necessary to a work of love and reconciliation? Have we shown ourselves so unwilling to be reconciled that force must be called in to win back our love? Let us not deceive ourselves, sir. These are the implements of war and subjugation; the last arguments to which kings resort. I ask gentlemen, sir, what means this martial array, if its purpose be not to force us to submission? Can gentlemen assign any other possible motive for it? Has Great Britain any enemy, in this quarter of the world, to call for all this accumulation of navies and armies? No, sir, she has none. They are meant for us: they can be meant for no other. They are sent over to bind and rivet upon us those chains which the British ministry have been so long forging. And what have we to oppose to them? Shall we try argument? Sir, we have been trying that for the last ten years. Have we anything new to offer upon the subject? Nothing. We have held the subject up in every light of which it is capable; but it has been all in vain. Shall we resort to entreaty and humble supplication? What terms shall we find which have not been already exhausted? Let us not, I beseech you, sir, deceive ourselves. Sir, we have done everything that could be done to avert the storm which is now coming on. We have petitioned; we have remonstrated; we have supplicated; we have prostrated ourselves before the throne, and have implored its interposition to arrest the tyrannical hands of the ministry and Parliament. Our petitions have been slighted; our remonstrances have produced additional violence and insult; our supplications have been disregarded; and we have been spurned, with contempt, from the foot of the throne! In vain, after these things, may we indulge the fond hope of peace and reconciliation. There is no longer any room for hope. If we wish to be free— if we mean to preserve inviolate those inestimable privileges for which we have been so long contending—if we mean not basely to abandon the noble struggle in which we have been so long engaged, and which we have pledged ourselves never to abandon until the glorious object of our contest shall be obtained—we must fight! I repeat it, sir, we must fight! An appeal to arms and to the God of hosts is all that is left us!

They tell us, sir, that we are weak; unable to cope with so formidable an adversary. But when shall we be stronger? Will it be the next week, or the next year? Will it be when we are totally disarmed, and when a British guard shall be stationed in every house? Shall we gather strength by irresolution and inaction? Shall we acquire the means of effectual resistance by lying supinely on our backs and hugging the delusive phantom of hope, until our enemies shall have bound us hand and foot? Sir, we are not weak if we make a proper use of those means which the God of nature hath placed in our power.

This last sentence gives direct credit to God for the powers on earth. This is another example of the Biblical influence.

The millions of people, armed in the holy cause of liberty, and in such a country as that which we possess, are invincible by any force which our enemy can send against us. Besides, sir, we shall not fight our battles alone. There is a just God who presides over the destinies of nations, and who will raise up friends to fight our battles for us.

Patrick Henry used second Chronicles 32:8 to illustrate his point in this last sentence. The direct Biblical text states,... with him is an arm of flesh; but with us is the lord our God, to help us and to fight our battles. Patrick Henry's next statement in his speech is very telling of a higher being.

The battle, sir, is not to the strong alone

The above sentence is also a direct reference to the Holy Scripture. This is reflected in Ecclesiastes 9:11. The direct passage from the Bible says, again I saw that under the sun the race is not to the swift, nor the battle to the strong, nor the bread to the wise, nor riches to the intelligent, nor favor to the men of skill but time and chance happen to them all.

it is to the vigilant, the active, the brave. Besides, sir, we have no election. If we were base enough to desire it, it is now too late to retire from the contest. There is no retreat but in submission and slavery! Our chains are forged! Their clanking may be heard on the plains of Boston! The war is inevitable— and let it come! I repeat it, sir, let it come. It is in vain, sir, to extenuate the matter. Gentlemen may cry, Peace, Peace— but there is no peace

This last sentence is once again referenced from the Bible. It is taken from Jeremiah 6:14. The full scripture says, They have healed the wounded of my people lightly, saying, 'Peace, 'peace,' when there is no peace.

the war is actually begun! The next gale that sweeps from the north will bring to our ears the clash of resounding arms! Our brethren are already in the field! Why stand we here idle?

This is the last sentence directly referenced in Patrick Henry's famous speech. It is a direct reference to Mathew 20:6. The passage reads, And about the eleventh hour he went out and found others standing; and he said to them. 'Why do you stand here idle all day?'

What is it that gentlemen wish? What would they have? Is life so dear, or peace so sweet, as to be purchased at the price of chains and slavery? Forbid it, Almighty God! I know not what course others may take; but as for me, give me liberty or give me death!

In 1765 Patrick Henry was elected to the Virginia House of Burgesses. In 1769 he was first admitted to the Bar of the General Court in Virginia. He was elected to the Continental Congress in 1774. Many people do not know that he served as a military leader in Virginia in 1775. He was also elected and served as Governor of Virginia from 1776 to 1778. Patrick Henry passed away at the age of 63, about the same age as William Paterson.

America's First Bible Society and National Bible Convention

The start of America's first Bible society was founded in 1809 by clergy members as well as Dr.Benjamin Rush. Dr. Rush position states that it is in living by the Bible that man becomes both "humanized and civilized."� To print the bible more cost-effectively and faster, they implemented the use of stereotyped printing. This method was a primitive way for the mass production of printed material. They were aided in gaining access to the Stereotype plates with the help of President James Madison and Congress. In the Capitol building is where Dr. Rush's Bible society obtained the stereotype plates for use in mass producing Bibles. The Maryland Bible society was founded by James McHenry signer of the Declaration of Independence. He said:

The Holy Scriptures can alone secure to society order and peace. And to our courts of justice and constitutions of governments purity, stability and usefulness. In vain, without the Bible, we increase our penal laws and draw protections around our institutions. Bibles are strong entrenchments. Where they abound men cannot purse wicked courses.

In 1816 the First national Bible society was founded called The American Bible society. The American Bible Society was founded in 1816. The leaders of the American Bible Society prove the solid connection between the Founding Fathers and the Bible. The list of the founding fathers involved in the American Bible Society is a very prominent list of founding members included Elias Boudinot, who was the President of the organization and former president of the Continental Congress. Additional Founding Fathers involved in the American Bible Society included: John Jay, John Quincy Adams, DeWitt Clinton and James Fennimore Cooper. Other influential men linked to the American Bible Society included: Rutherford B. Hayes, Benjamin Harrison and Francis Scott Key. Since those early days, American Bible Society has worked closely with organizations to reach people in the United States and around the world who might otherwise not have access to a Bible. 'John Jay who was the original Chief-Justice of the U. S.

Supreme Court, and the president of the American Bible Association said,

The Bible... is the best of all books, for it is the word of God and teaches us the way to be happy in this world and in the next. Continue therefore to read it and to regulate your life by its precepts.

Conclusion

There were many instrumental people in the founding of America, many of whom will never receive credit. The Founding Fathers were clearly the direction and leadership that the United States needed in the formation of such a young and fledgling country. Had it not been for the courageous leadership and brilliant minds of these great men, not only would the United States not be a leader of the world but the world as we know it could have been dramatically different over the past 250 years. The Founding Fathers having used the experiences and education they had developed over the years, which culminated in the ability of these great men to work as a team to form the doctrine of the greatest nation in the world. It is extremely amazing the talent and ability these great men had, moreover; having it all culminate at the right time in history.

As one researches and looks at the brilliance of these men and the time and effort exerted one should come to believe and understand that our founders and the creation of the United States was a product of a divine being, the Lord. In no other culture has the doctrine of the spirit of Christianity and law worked together in such as harmonious fashion to create the best form of government the world has ever known. The influence of the Founding Fathers doctrine of Christianity is one of the leading factors in the development of such a great form of government, since no other country has been formed out of such a doctrine and not been as successful. The Founding Fathers that were included in this research paper are just a small fraction of the total number of Founding Fathers that believed in the doctrine of a higher being and the necessity to use their personal beliefs in the Lord as the basis for their actions and formations of the United States of America. Clearly in the example and writing from the above Founding Fathers in this research paper, the examples of their thoughts and beliefs of the necessity of the Lord can be seen in many different cases. There are over 15,000 references used in the Founding Fathers writings and speeches that mention the Lord or a higher power. The claim that the Founding Fathers were deists is a false premise based on the majority of the founders. There are a few Founding Fathers that would be classified as deists but the overwhelming majority of the founders based on their own writing, speeches, diaries and personal letters clearly shows that they believed there was a divine intervention that a higher power played an instrumental role in the continued success and development of the United States.

The ideological beliefs of the Founding Fathers are and should continue to be the exemplary doctrine in the continued success of what started this nation and made this country the most successful in History. "In my opinion, "a nation, like America, which despite all odds of prior history should continue the fundamental practice that clearly has paved the way for these great states as being a divine and blessed country."

2
References

[1] Michael J Chapman, <u>Testimony on the American Heritage Act</u> (www.AmericanHeritageResearch.com)

[1] Edmund S Morgan, <u>The Puritan Dilemma</u> (Little, brown and Company) Longman Paperback, 3rd Edition, 224 pages, 2006)

[1] http://teachers.henrico.k12.va.us/fairfield/saunders_d/homework/colonies/puritans.pdf

[1] Houston Baptist University, <u>The Bible in America University</u> (Houston, TX: Houston Baptist University, Vol 2, Issue 1, October 2004, Pg 1)

[1] General Court of Connecticut, <u>The Code of 1650</u> (Hartford: Silas Andrus 1822), 92-93. (The old Deluder act: From Records of the Governor and Company of the Massachusetts bay in New England, II: 203)

References

[1] Harris, Benjamin. The New England Primer. Aledo, Texas: Wallbuilder press, 2010.

[1] Journal of the continental Congress, 1774 to 1789 (Washington, DC: Government Printing office, 1904), Vol. I, pp26, September 6-7, 1774.

[1] George L Clark, A Connecticut leader in the American Revolution (New York, G.P. Putnam's Son, 1913), 11

[1] John Adams, Letter to wife (Edited by his Grandson, Charles Francis Adams, Volume 1, 1841) http://www.familytales.org/dbDisplay.php?id=ltr_jod2809&person=jod

[1] Abram E. Brown, *John Hancock: His Book* (Boston: Lee and Shepard Publishers, 1898), p. 269, Hancock's Inaugural Address as Governor of Massachusetts, 1780

[1] Ibid

[1] Thomas Jefferson, *The Writings of Thomas Jefferson* (Washington D. C.: The Thomas Jefferson Memorial Association, 1904), Vol. XIII, p. 292-294. In a letter from John Adams to Thomas Jefferson on June 28, 1813.

[1] http://www.usconstitution.net/parispeace.html

[1] Lester J. Cappon, ed., *The Adams-Jefferson Letters The Complete Correspondence between Thomas Jefferson and Abigail and John Adams*(The University of North Carolina Press 1959), 5.

[1] Benjamin Rush M.D., <u>*Essays, Literary, Moral & Philosophical*</u> (Philadelphia: Printed by Thomas and Samuel F. Bradford, 1798. Pg 93

[1] Columbia Electronic Encyclopedia, 6th Edition,**Paine,RobertTreat**, 1731–1814 (New York New York: Columbia University Press.

[1]http://benjaminrush.org/seattleartmuseum.aspx

[1]Hanson, editors (Boston: Massachusetts Historical Society, 1992), Vol. I, p. 48, Robert Treat Paine's Confession of Faith, 1749.)

[1] Columbia Electronic Encyclopedia, 6th Edition,**Paine,RobertTreat**, 1731–1814 (New York New York: Columbia University Press

[1] Colonialhall.com

[1] http://charlescarrollhouse.org/

[1] From an autographed letter in our (our refers to the possession of David Barton) possession written by Charles

Carroll to Charles W. Wharton, Esq., on September 27, 1825, from Doughoragen, Maryland.

[1] Source: Bernard C. Steiner, *The Life and Correspondence of James McHenry* (Cleveland: The Burrows Brothers, 1907), p. 475. In a letter from Charles Carroll to James McHenry of November 4, 1800.

[1] [1] Holmes, L. David. The Faith of the Founding Fathers. New York: Oxford Press, 2006. pg 20

[1] Lossing, B.J. Lives of the Signers of the Declaration of Independence. Aledo, Texas: Wallbuilder press,1995. pg81-82

[1] *The Works of John Witherspoon, (Edinburgh: J. Ogle, 1815), Vol. IV, p. 265, "Sermon Delivered at Public Thanksgiving After Peace"*

[1] *The Works of John Witherspoon*, (Edinburgh: J. Ogle, 1815), Vol. VII, pp. 139-140, 142, from his "Lectures on Moral Philosophy", Lecture 16 on "Oaths and Vows"

[1] Lossing, B.J. Lives of the Signers of the Declaration of Independence. Aledo, Texas: Wallbuilder press,1995.pg83

[1] http://www.mountvernon.org/content/timeline

[1] Holmes, L. David. The Faith of the Founding Fathers. New York: Oxford Press, 2006.pg 59

[1]http://www.restore-christian-america.org/founders.html

George Washington's prayer at Valley Forge.

[1] James Abercrombie, quoted in Paul Boller, George Washington and Religion(Dallas: Southern Methodist University press, 1963), pg 18.

[1] John Jay, The Correspondence and Public papers of John Jay, ed. Henry P. Johnston, 4 Vols.(New York: Burt Franklin, 1970), 3: 381.

[1] The prayer was written by Washington at Newburgh, New York, at the close of the Revolutionary War on June 14, 1783. It was sent to the thirteen governors of the newly freed states in a "Circular Letter Addressed to the Governors of all the States on the Disbanding of the Army."

[1] Johnstone, Williams. George Washington the Christian. New York: Abrington Press, 1919. Pg28-29

[1] http://baltimore.org/arts-and-culture/fort-mchenry

[1](Source: Bernard C. Steiner, *One Hundred and Ten Years of BibleSociety Work in Maryland, 1810-1920* (Maryland BibleSociety, 1921), p. 14.)

References

[1]http://www.archives.gov/exhibits/charters/constitution_founding_fathers_maryland.html#McHenry

[1] http://www.archives.gov/exhibits/charters/constitution_founding_fathers_maryland.html

[1] http://www.georgiaencyclopedia.org/nge/Article.jsp?id=h-2710

[1] *"Biographical Sketches of the Delegates from Georgia to the Continental Congress"*, Charles C. Jones, (Boston and New York: Houghton, Mifflin and Company, 1891), pp. 6-7

[1] www.georgiaencyclopedia.org/nge/Article.jsp?id=h-2710

[1]http://www.libs.uga.edu/hargrett/archives/exhibit/charter/chartertranscription.html

[1]http://www.libs.uga.edu/hargrett/archives/exhibit/charter/chartertranscription.html

[1] www.georgiaencyclopedia.org/nge/Article.jsp?id=h-2710

[1] http://dictionary.reference.com/browse/deism
[1] *United States Founding Father, Signer and Penman of the Constitution, Gouverneur Morris, "Collections of the New York historical Society for the Year 1821", (New York: E. Bliss and E. White, 1821), p. 30, from "An Inaugural Discourse Delivered Before the New York Historical Society by the Honorable Gouverneur Morris", September 4, 1816*

[1] http://dictionary.reference.com/browse/deism
[1] *"The Life of Governeur Morris", Jared Sparks, (Boston: Gray and Bowen, 1832), Vol. III, p. 483, from his "Notes on the Form of a Constitution for France"*

[1] *United States Founding Father, Signer and Penman of the Constitution, Gouverneur Morris, "A Diary of the French Revolution", (Boston: Houghton Mifflin Co., 1939), Vol. II, p. 172, April 29, 1791; Vol. II, p. 452, to Lord George Gordon, June 28, 1792*

[1] http://www.whitehouse.gov/our-government/the-constitution

[1] http://colonialhall.com/morrisg/morrisg.php

[1]http://www.constitutionfacts.com/?section=declaration&page=aboutTheSigners.cfm

[1]http://www.archives.gov/exhibits/charters/constitution_founding_fathers_new_jersey.html#Paterson

[1] This is the text of the November 21, 1791 William Paterson Thanksgiving Day proclamation, as he served as governor of New Jersey; as printed in the *Gazette of the United States*, November 26, 1791.

[1] Holmes, L. David. <u>The Faith of the Founding Fathers</u>. New York: Oxford Press, 2006.pg 141

[1] <u>The Holy Bible</u>, Revised Standard Version. New York: Thomas Nelson and Sons, 1952. Pg 789

[1] [1] <u>The Holy Bible</u>, Revised Standard Version. New York: Thomas Nelson and Sons, 1952. Pg 34

[1] <u>The Holy Bible</u>, Revised Standard Version. New York: Thomas Nelson and Sons, 1952. Pg 482

[1] <u>The Holy Bible</u>, Revised Standard Version. New York: Thomas Nelson and Sons, 1952. Pg 700

[1] <u>The Holy Bible</u>, Revised Standard Version. New York: Thomas Nelson and Sons, 1952. Pg 790

[1] <u>The Holy Bible</u>, Revised Standard Version. New York: Thomas Nelson and Sons, 1952. Pg 24

References

[1] http://www.wallbuilders.com/LIBissuesArticles.asp?id=54

[1] http://www.ushistory.org/declaration/related/henry.htm

[1] http://www.archives.gov/exhibits/charters/constitution_founding_fathers_new_jersey.html#Paterson

[1] http://davidbartonblog.weebly.com/1/previous/3.html

[1] http://vftonline.org/EndTheWall/magna_charta.htm

[1] http://www.americanbible.org/about/history

[1] http://www.free2pray.info/5founderquotes.html

www.ingramcontent.com/pod-product-compliance
Lightning Source LLC
Chambersburg PA
CBHW031455040426
42444CB00007B/1105